Radical Notes 2

NEOLIBERALISM AND HINDUTVA

Fascism, Free Markets and the Restructuring of Indian Capitalism

Series Editors

Pratyush Chandra

Pothik Ghosh

Ravi Kumar

Saswat Pattanayak

Radical Notes 2

Neoliberalism and Hindutva

Fascism, Free Markets and the Restructuring of Indian Capitalism

Shankar Gopalakrishnan

AAKAR

NEOLIBERALISM AND HINDUTVA
Shankar Gopalakrishnan

radicalnotes@radicalnotes.com

First Published, 2009

ISBN 978-81-89833-80-0

Published by
AAKAR BOOKS
28 E Pocket IV, Mayur Vihar Phase I, Delhi-110 091
Phone : 011-2279 5505 Telefax : 011-2279 5641
aakarbooks@gmail.com; www.aakarbooks.com

Printed at
Sapra Brothers, Delhi 110 092

A movement in a sense is a struggle over the definition of reality—how reality is constituted. It is this struggle that builds the focus and targets of the movement, informing the praxes towards social transformation. Inherent in this struggle is the act of reclaiming—sense and sensibility, words and meaning...

The word "radical", which in this post-Cold War phase of Global Capitalism or globaloney has been reduced to a general notion characterizing all kinds of extremism and deviance, is one such word that has been time and again reclaimed by the practitioners of social transformation. "Radical" derived from the Latin word, 'radix' meaning 'root' = 'basic' = 'fundamental' is a concept that aptly defines a transformatory practice as an endeavour to reveal and target the essence of what is given to us in appearance. Radicalism in this sense is nothing but fundamental transformation rather than politicking in appearances. Further, and foremost, it is the all-round critique of the status quo and its genealogies, rather than accepting the disciplinary divide/boundaries that the capitalist system perpetuates in order to control labour-power and labour, our efforts and their fruits.

Radical Notes is an endeavour to coordinate the radical voices around the globe, with special focus on South Asia. In our view such focus (which could have been anything) is not just for convenience, given the facilitators' cultural and intellectual comfort, but is also needed to concretise any 'radical' pursuit. In our view South Asia provides us the opportunity to visualize the reproduction of 'global' capitalism and struggle against it in a regional setting. But we must remember such focus is always fluid with the ever-dynamic radical needs of the humanity.

Radical Notes booklets are contributions on social, cultural, political or economic issues from counter-hegemonic perspectives, which need not be confined to any established socialist and communist current of thought (though these approaches are most welcome).

Series Editors
Radical Notes

Contents

1

INTRODUCTION

Over the 1980s and 1990s we witnessed the simultaneous rise of two reactionary political projects, Hindutva and neoliberalism, to a position of dominance in India. Such a combination is not unusual, in that neoliberalism is usually allied with and promoted by socially reactionary forces (such as the hyper-nationalism of the "bureaucratic-authoritarian" dictatorships in Latin America, the implicit racism and jingoism of Thatcher and Reagan, etc.). Yet the Indian experience, while sharing this broad tendency, also contains some very distinct characteristics.

We on the left have tended to understand this simultaneous rise as a straightforward cause-effect relationship. Hindutva is seen as an effort by neoliberalism, or perhaps more broadly by capitalism, to divert attention from class conflict, to divide and weaken working class struggles and to deflect class-driven anxieties on to minority communities. This approach is problematic in two senses. First, it does not explain why Hindutva organisations are able to develop a mass base, except to the extent that they are seen to be appealing to "historical identity" or "emotive" issues. This is undoubtedly true. But it is also insufficient, for by definition any right wing project will appeal to "emotions"; it does not take our understanding of the actual appeal of Hindutva forward. Second, it fails to provide us much understanding of why this specific historical conjuncture has taken place. Hindutva is seen as simply an "available" reactionary ideology that capital has picked up for its purposes.

In this context, this paper attempts a sketch of a different approach. I seek to argue that, for reasons specific to Indian capitalism at this historical moment, what we might call the *political projects* of Hindutva and neoliberalism share certain socio-political agendas. This shared agenda extends at times to a tactical alliance of the two, where both seek to exploit their "common ground" in order to achieve a restructuring of the Indian polity. Moreover, this alliance has already had a considerable impact on large parts of the discursive and political landscape of India - an impact that has not yet been seriously challenged.

It should be noted that my argument here is neither that this shared agenda was inevitable, nor that it precludes alliances between neoliberalism and other political forces in India. The analysis postulates that this is a historically specific development, shaped by political circumstances, the current balance of forces and the choices made by political actors. Yet, this is also not an alliance based purely on expediency. These projects have shared a *logic* whose validity is not infinite - in the sense that it will eventually break down under the weight of its contradictions - but is also not entirely non-existent.[1]

1. This paper builds on the arguments made in an earlier paper (Gopalakrishnan 2006) but also modifies and attempts to place those arguments in a larger context.

2

THEORETICAL APPROACH

Poulantzas' Concept of Individualisation

This paper draws on three different theoretical concepts for its argument. The first is Nicos Poulantzas' (1978) analysis of the relationship between capitalist states and "individualisation." Incorporating Foucault's analysis into a Marxist framework, he argues that the capitalist state constructs a concept of the "individual" - the "juridical-political person" - as an isolated entity, identical to all other individuals but disconnected from them, whose only connection/unity is represented by the state. As he puts it, the "centralised, bureaucratised State installs this atomization and, as a representative State laying claim to national sovereignty and the popular will, it represents the unity of a body (people-nation) that is split into formally equivalent monads."

The projection of the "individual" is not merely an automatic reflection of the fact that capitalist society is built around commodity relations. Rather, the dispossession of the producer and the creation of capitalist relations of production generate a "material frame of reference" that makes the individual the centre point of social relations. The state, in turn, "inscribes itself" into this frame of reference, representing both the frame's ideological unity - the "nation-state" - and its system of organization/regulation. In this sense, it is the state that in fact *realises* the material frame of reference and gives it social substance. The state then actively participates in perpetuating this situation by constantly constructing and reconstructing the "individual." "Individualisation constitutes the material expression in capitalist bodies of the existing relations of production and the social division of labour; and it is equally the material effect of state practices and techniques forging and subordinating this (political) body."

Thus, creating and projecting the "individual" is the centre of the active process by which capitalist relations of production are *constituted and reconstituted* by the capitalist state. As a result, the concept of the individual becomes "the original ground of classes in their capitalist specificity." The "individual" forms the conceptual terrain on which class relationships within capitalism are defined.

Poulantzas' argument, however, assumes that this process is complete in all existing capitalist democratic states. What happens when this remains incomplete? Can the individualisation process itself become a site of social struggle? These questions form the basis for some of the explorations here.

Hegemony

The second analysis that is drawn upon is Gramsci's familiar concept of "hegemony", the combination of force with "intellectual and moral leadership" that builds the sense that the ruling "historical bloc" (of one or multiple class fractions) represents the "general interest." As Gramsci (1971) says, "the dominant group is coordinated concretely with the general interests of the subordinate groups, and the life of the State is conceived of as a continuous process of formation and superseding of unstable equilibria (on the juridical plane) between the interests of the fundamental group and those of the subordinate groups - equilibria in which the interests of the dominant group prevail, but only up to a certain point, i.e. stopping short of narrowly corporate economic interest."

Three aspects of the concept of hegemony will be critical to our analysis here. First, hegemony is never total, and always contains within itself instabilities and contradictions. Maintaining hegemony requires a constant effort by the ruling bloc: "the maintenance of hegemony involves taking systematic account of popular interests and demands, shifting position and making compromises ... to maintain support and alliances"[2].

Second, hegemony is not simply deceit. Rather, it is *material and concrete*. It is built around channelling genuine social contradictions in a manner that supports the continued dominance of the ruling bloc. This is naturally impossible to fully achieve, and it is for this reason that hegemony is partial and unstable. If we look at hegemony this way, the analytical focus shifts away from whether a particular ideological project is "false" or is geared towards dividing and weakening the working class or the oppressed. Indeed, both these statements would be true of any ruling class political project. Rather, to understand the functioning of hegemony, analysis would focus on the process by which the interests of the subordinate classes are *coordinated* with those of the ruling bloc.

Third, implicit in Gramsci's analysis is that the generation of hegemony is neither an automatic nor a spontaneous process. Hegemony is instead the result of conscious political action by an organised formation - the "totalitarian" party. In The *Modern Prince* (1971), Gramsci describes a "totalitarian" party as one that seeks to replace the state as the "neutral body" of society.[3] It attempts to build a hegemonic "national-popular" will whereby it identifies the interests of its leading class with those of the rest of society. Analysing such a party requires understanding first the objective social forces that it is responding to, followed by the degree and nature of self-understanding of its leading classes. The most "political phase" in any such party's development is reached when it succeeds in "posing all the questions around which the struggle rages not on a corporate but on a 'universal' plane, and thus creating the hegemony of a fundamental social group over a series of subordinate groups." It is important to note that this method

2. Jessop (1982).
3. The term "totalitarian" is used by Gramsci's translators as it is the most direct equivalent of the Italian term. However, the term is not meant to carry the negative implications or historical allusions to Nazism that it carries in English.

of analysis does not require that the party succeed in creating this hegemony - only that it attempts to do so.

Petty Commodity Production

The third concept relied upon here is that of the existence and persistence of what has variously been called "petty commodity production" (Bernstein 2001), or "non-capitalist commodity production"[4]. In this case, unlike in "pure" capitalist production relations, the "agents of this form of production are capitalists and workers at the same time because they own or have access to means of production and employ their own labour" (Bernstein 2001). Such production is by no means "outside" capitalism. It is first and foremost *commodity* production, in that it is production shaped as part of a commodity and market relationship, and such producers are dependent on commodity relationships for survival. It is therefore shaped, controlled and in some measure produced by capitalism, and is an integral part of the capitalist social formation. Moreover, as Bernstein (2003) emphasises elsewhere, the role that such production plays in the social division of labour is generally in flux. Spaces for petty commodity production are continually created, destroyed and recreated within the capitalist formation.

It might be objected that this is in no way a new conception. Marxist analysis has long used the term "petty bourgeois" to refer to what seems a similar class. That term is consciously avoided here for two reasons. First, it has now become

4. Personal communication from Suhas Paranjape. Paranjape also describes two other spheres of production - household and subsistence - that are also very much a part of contemporary capitalist societies, but do not themselves rely on "pure" capitalist relations of production. It should be noted that the term "petty commodity production" is used here to avoid the confusion induced by the term "non-capitalist commodity production", which seems to imply that this form of production is "external" to capitalism. But the former term is also somewhat misleading, in that such production is not "petty" in any physical sense - neither at an individual level nor in terms of its role in the larger social formation.

analytically imprecise and has been applied across the board to many social sectors, some of whom would overlap with petty commodity production and some of whom would not. Second, it is generally considered a "transitional" class, a residual in the social formation. However, Bernstein, Paranjape and a growing body of other Marxist literature has highlighted the reproduction and at times expansion of petty commodity production as a key aspect of modern capitalism.

Finally, the focus here on petty commodity producers is not intended to imply that such producers are not "workers" or that petty commodity production is not, for many such producers, a form of disguised wage labour. It is aimed rather at examining the political implications of such forms of production within Indian capitalism, and their interaction with attempts at constructing hegemonic projects in the Indian polity.

3

INDIAN CAPITALISM AND PETTY COMMODITY PRODUCTION

Petty commodity production clearly plays a major role in the Indian economy (though it is no longer the major site of capital accumulation). Census data shows a consistent pattern of a majority of Indians reporting themselves as "self-employed", a category which would largely overlap with petty commodity producers in the sense described above. The vast majority of landholding agriculturists in particular fall within this category, excepting a small minority of capitalist farmers. In urban areas, most small enterprises share these characteristics.

Such petty commodity production is constantly subjected to the pressure of class differentiation. In agricultural areas, poor peasants face a reproduction squeeze that drives them further and further into proletarianisation. The small number of rich peasants - until the neoliberal era - aspired, and in some areas succeeded, in making the transition to agricultural capitalism. Similar tendencies operate in urban areas. Such pressures have however not destroyed petty commodity production as a sector of the capitalist economy, a state of affairs that is in fact true of peasantries around the world.[5]

The Indian economy thus can be described as a capitalist economy where the majority of people exist in class positions shaped, if not necessarily defined, by petty commodity

5. Bernstein (2001, 2003).

production. This state of affairs is generally seen as an outcome of the historical legacy of distorted capitalism and colonial intervention. In addition, however, there is a proximate cause, in the form of conscious state policy and political action in the decades since Independence. Indeed, if we adopt a heterodox reading of India's planned economy, it could be argued that a major goal of state policy has been to shape the relationship between capital and petty commodity production in India - and that part of this shaping has been a dual relationship of "shielding" and deliberate subordination of petty commodity production.

Partha Chatterjee (1998) and Corbridge and Harriss (2000) have argued that the planned mixed economy was a "passive revolution" initiated by the Indian bourgeoisie, a result of its inability to tackle the continued power of the landlord classes in the first decades after Independence. Certain elements of these policies, many of which still continue, had a clear relevance not only to the landlord classes but to spheres of petty commodity production. Some measures appeared intended to "protect" and perpetuate these systems of production: for instance, reservations for small-scale industries, the peculiarities and numerical limits of Indian labour law, some aspects of priority sector lending and the promotion of cooperatives. These had the net effect of erecting barriers to transformation into capitalist enterprises, hence encouraging capital and most producers to either disguise themselves as petty commodity producers or engage in 'outsourcing' of production to such producers. Yet, simultaneously, various other mechanisms operated to ensure the continued extraction of surplus from such sectors: unequal exchange through agricultural price fixing, the relative failure of institutional lending, the allocation of space in urban areas, etc. Such surplus extraction at times shaded into the forms now described as "accumulation by dispossession" (Harvey 2003), but not to the extent of threatening the continued existence of petty commodity production.

The result has been an active state contribution to the perpetuation of a large but dominated sphere of petty commodity production. The reason why this occurred is out of my scope here, but for the purposes of our present argument it is sufficient to consider its consequences for India's polity. In particular, the persistence of petty commodity production has been a major contributing factor - though not the sole one - in the prominence of "social structures of accumulation", namely institutions such as caste, gender, religious community, geography and kinship networks, in the regulation of Indian capitalism (Harriss-White 2003). Indeed, petty commodity production in India is marked by the relative absence of direct, formal state intervention in most production processes. State action plays a key role in shaping such production, but does so indirectly, or at times "perversely."

One key result of such processes is that the tendency towards *individualisation,* which Poulantzas identifies as central to the function of the capitalist state, has always been highly contested, incomplete and dysfunctional in the Indian context. The construction of the "individual" as the isolated but identical monad exists in a kind of continual dialectical battle with other concepts of social actors and social relations. This impact is not limited only to those engaged in commodity production or who have access to means of production. "Workers" - in the limited sense of those with little or no access to means of production at all[6] - find wage employment overwhelmingly with those who are themselves petty commodity producers, and hence they too are integrated into the ideological-material-regulatory complex that marks such production in India.

Since the concept of the individual is central to the definition of social relations in a capitalist state, this in turn has had an impact on the ground of political struggle around class in India. As Harriss-White and Gooptu (2001) put it in the context of unorganised sector labour, in India the struggle of workers is as much a "struggle over class" as it is a "struggle between classes." The same can be extended to the struggles of most petty commodity producers. The large-scale presence of petty

6. As said earlier, many petty commodity producers are effectively engaged in disguised wage labour in any case.

commodity production thus feeds into the domination of the Indian political scene by political forces consisting of "cross-class" alliances (commonly described as "populist" in left analyses).

4

THE MOVEMENT OF THE 1980s

Against this background, one can attempt a historical analysis of the rise of Hindutva and neoliberalism. The analysis here begins with the decade of the 1980s. As both an ideological tendency and as an organised political force, Hindutva is of course far older than this decade. But it is in these years that it emerged as a dominant mass force in Indian politics. Similarly, while there have liberalist ideological tendencies in some fringe elements of Indian politics from Independence onwards, liberalism - and, post 1991, neoliberalism - emerges as a powerful political project in India only in this decade.

Why might this have been the case? The 1980s were a period of major upheaval in the Indian polity, witnessing an upsurge of new political forces. These included the "social movements", the new regional parties, the armed uprisings in several major areas of India's periphery (Kashmir, Assam, and Punjab) and eventually the Mandal mobilisations. In some ways these mobilisations shared nothing in common except that they exploded into the "vacuum" left by the declining coherence of the Indian state and the Congress party. Yet the largest of the movements in the Indian mainland - the regional parties, the "new farmers' movements" and the Mandal mobilisations - did have one common characteristic. This was the dominant, or at least leading, presence of "rich peasant" groups.

Zamindari abolition and the Green Revolution had contributed by the early 1980s to the creation of a small class of capitalist farmers and a larger, though less clearly defined, class of 'rich farmers' in most States in India (excepting the

Northeast). The impact of such trends was already visible in the fragmentation and organisational decline of the Congress from the late 1960s (Vanaik 1990). In the 1980s, these classes formed the bedrock of regional parties such as the TDP, the INLD, the SAD or the Samajwadi Party, as well as the leading sections of both the farmers' movements and the subsequent OBC mobilisations.

In the terms of the argument here, these were social groups at the upper end of petty commodity production, often either having become fully capitalist or on the verge of doing so. These groups faced two primary problems in the 1980s. First, the gradual shift in terms of trade against agriculture through the decade threatened their ability to transition to capitalist agriculture, and in some cases even their ability to reproduce their current conditions of existence. Second, the rise of these communities was not reflected in a concomitant change in political power–which remained in the hands of the urban bourgeoisie.

Simultaneously, other petty commodity producers were subject to an increasing reproduction squeeze, as the state loosened its controls on big capital at precisely the time when their dependence on the market had increased (see below and Bernstein 2001). The "new farmers' movements" offer a clear illustration of the result. For instance the Shetkari Sanghatna, the largest "new farmers movement" after Tikait's, built its entire mobilisation on the question of agricultural prices. Though led and dominated by rich peasants, this organisation succeeded in building a mass base among middle and even poorer peasants through its advocacy of higher prices (Dhanagare 1995). This issue concerned most agricultural petty commodity producers, even those who might be net purchasers of agricultural goods, for it defined their relationship with the market economy - a relationship that had become increasingly precarious. Though the Sanghatna leadership explicitly claimed to be in favour of a withdrawal of the state from agricultural and the end of "socialist" regulation on agricultural production, its entire mobilisational universe was built around the assumption of state regulation of prices. When such state regulation did indeed collapse after 1991, the organisation effectively collapsed shortly afterwards.

While such demands were rarely so clearly stated elsewhere, one theme remained: based on a perception of shared interests across petty commodity producers, the parties/ movements/organisations demanded that the state allocate more resources, subsidies, and other such supports to their forms of production - and particularly their rich farmer classes. This was converted into logics that made sense across the spectrum of petty commodity production, affected as it was in varying degrees by state investment and regulation. This demand for a "tilt" in the state machinery proved effective at mobilising large sections of petty commodity producers, generating powerful political "waves" that swept aside the Congress in much of mainland India.

Each of these political formations foregrounded the state as the main target of its demands, and thus implicitly as the agent of social transformation - while simultaneously weakening faith in the ability of the state to deliver on these demands. Moreover, the discourse around the state presented it as an arbiter between the interests of *communities*: a "populist" concept that gained a material foundation through the common interests of petty commodity producers.

Meanwhile, as the state and the Congress party weakened under these demands, other movements - such as the Dalit and tribal movements - also expanded and grew. Many of these other organisations used the same vocabulary as the larger organisations, reinforcing this conceptual framework as the "common sense" of Indian politics.

Regulations on Capital in the 1980s

Simultaneously, however, the other side of this equation was also changing. Until the 1970s, India's big bourgeoisie had built monopolistic large corporations through a symbiotic relationship with the state bureaucracy, relying on state regulation to provide them with captive markets. Now, these capitals also began to chafe at the state system, with the continued small size of their markets becoming an obstacle to their growth. State regulation also blocked them from easily absorbing smaller capitals and non-capitalist commodity producers. The post-1980 Congress regime gradually began to change regulatory policies in order to meet this demand. In 1985 the government promulgated a "New Economic Policy", with tax cuts, lower import duties, export tax breaks and relaxed licensing requirements. The result was a boom in growth, which in turn pushed the Indian economy into a higher growth cycle that it has - on average - maintained ever since (Corbridge and Harriss 2000, Rodrik and Subramaniam 2004).

These two simultaneous but contradictory trends - an increase in demands on the state machinery for support to petty commodity producers, and pressure to relax its restraints on capital - led to an unusual economic conjuncture. As the economy entered its "boom" period, state expenditure and deficit financing also rose greatly, resulting in a rapid rise in rural investment. Rural employment grew, agricultural real wages rose, and income poverty decreased at a more rapid rate than either before or since (Ghosh and Chandrasekhar 2000). This 'boom' however was highly vulnerable, built around borrowing from NRI's and local sources. The resulting dependence on external finance capital was sufficient to trigger the 1991 "crisis", where sudden withdrawal of volatile funds led to a balance of payments crunch. This "crisis" - generated through capital flight - provided neoliberalism with its entry point, which we will return to below.

5

HINDUTVA AS A DOMINANT CLASS PROJECT

It was in this context of general 'prosperity', between roughly 1985 and 1992, that the Hindutva organisations undertook an incredibly rapid mass expansion. In 1984, the Sangh Parivar was still a relatively marginal entity, riding on the dying halo of the JP movement. By 1992, it could stake a credible claim to being India's largest organised political force[7], and the spectre of fascism was haunting the country. Such an extraordinary growth is unmatched by any other political force in independent India's history.

In itself, this historical conjuncture should make one doubt theories that seek to explain Hindutva as a "distraction" from the "distress" of the working class. Nor is it a response to a crisis of capitalism, as is sometimes argued by analogy with theories of classical European fascism. On the face of it, the economic evidence shows neither crisis nor an absolute increase in distress among the poor or the working class. Indeed, it shows the opposite. The rise of the Sangh hence cannot be reduced to, or simply read off from, the prevailing economic circumstances.

Such an explanation however requires a shift in emphasis from analyses of Hindutva as a predominantly *cultural-*

7. The Congress may at the time have had more members than the BJP, but it is doubtful that the Congress and its fronts could together match the numbers of the Sangh Parivar as a whole.

ideological phenomenon, which has been the most common approach taken by its opponents. Such analyses focus on the ideological aspects of "Hindu nationalism", approaching it by asking questions regarding the appeal of such reactionary chauvinism in this political conjuncture. This helps analyse the mass appeal of Hindutva, and also provides ammunition to counter its propaganda and hate politics. But it does not necessarily completely explain the actual growth of the Sangh Parivar. The Sangh Parivar is not merely a vehicle of Hindu chauvinism - it is the most successful political organisation in India today. Its expansion has been the result of conscious political action, not merely automatic or unconscious cultural propagation. Indeed, the Parivar is an excellent example of a "totalitarian party", in the Gramscian sense explored above. The growth of Hindutva is inseparable from the growth of the Parivar as an organisation.

From this angle, the Sangh has to be analysed as a *party*. It is necessary to look the manner in which the Parivar translates the dominant class interests that it projects into "universal" interests of other social sectors. This question turns also crucially on the manner in which the Sangh organises itself, for it is through such operations - as argued below - that it projects its actions as a response to social contradictions. This approach neither replaces nor negates the importance of deconstructing the hate politics of Hindutva; rather, it aims to complement it.

The Appeal of the Sangh Parivar to Dominant Class Interests

From the days of the Jan Sangh until the early 1980s, the Sangh Parivar had a relatively clearly defined mass base. The Jan Sangh, and then the BJP, was described as the "brahmin-baniya party", with little following in rural areas and an inability to capture either the support of urban elites or the working class. Its party positions were a fairly direct reflection of the class position of its supporters, mainly members of the trading class. It favoured external protectionism and internal trade liberalisation, reflecting its members' interests in unfettered access to domestic markets combined with restrictions on international competition. It opposed trade unions and workers' struggles and promoted reactionary and jingoistic nationalism. In this sense it was indeed a "petty bourgeois" party in the usual sense. Outside the party, the Sangh Parivar had established most of its current front organisations by the early 1960s, but they remained small.

The Parivar underwent its first wave of post independence growth, both in membership and in stature, during the JP movement, sharing in the popular anti-Emergency sentiment. But it was only in the 1980s that it truly emerged to become a major political force among the country's elite and big capital. Simultaneously, and primarily through the Ayodhya movement, it grew into a huge mass force.

At this time, there were some obvious benefits to capital in supporting Hindutva mobilisation. Many of these have already been discussed extensively in the literature. Ideologically, Hindutva was an antidote to the "subaltern" mobilisations of Mandal and the regional parties. It delegitimised class and caste struggle and instead promoted notions of "harmony." It is in this sense that Corbridge and Harriss (2000) have identified Hindutva as an "elite revolt" against the other mobilisations.

However, there is arguably a further element in the appeal that the Sangh Parivar enjoyed among the ruling class bloc - one which was specifically important in this time. The other movements of the time projected a politics of "communities" competing for state resources and control of the state machinery. Such politics had the effect, at the national level, of further contesting and undermining any effort at individualisation in the Indian polity. It explicitly foregrounded the notion that the polity of the country was a fractured one, built not around identical monads finding their unity in the state, but on contesting, frequently internally divided communities. In this manner it was indeed a class contestation - though a partial and contradictory one - rooted in the particular positions of petty commodity producers.

This was not a threat to Indian capital as such. As said earlier, individualisation has been a contested process throughout India's recent history, and moreover petty commodity production - and the ideological systems associated with it - is a fundamental feature of Indian capitalism. Yet, it is arguable that the particular type of contestation witnessed in the 1980s was seen as a challenge. It was during this period, particularly the second half of the decade, that big capital in India had begun to push for opportunities to expand into new markets. The "reforms" of the mid 1980s served precisely this purpose. But, the contestation of individualisation embodied in the other movements of this decade threatened the coherence of the national state, whose active intervention was increasingly vital for such "reforms." Indeed, these movements demanded precisely the kind of state action that capital increasingly found anathema - increased segmentation of markets, dictation of state spending by democratic politics and state interference in decisions by private capitalists. Finally, expansion by capital in this period also depended on cultural-ideological factors such as a common understanding of unified markets and commodity exchange in rural areas. This was an understanding that was lacking at the time (Rajagopal 1999), and was directly threatened by the promotion of community identities.

It is in this context that a much deeper appeal of Hindutva becomes apparent. To see this, let us examine some of the internal elements of Hindutva ideology, and in particular its approach to its own cadre and supporters. This approach is in no sense limited to merely anti-minority hate politics. Rather, it contains a very specific concept of the relationship between *individual, society and state,* an approach that is of particular interest in light of the prevailing political situation. Some of the key elements of this are as follows[8]:

- *Reduction of social processes to individual choice*: Like most organicist ideologies (and in a strong parallel to Gandhianism), Hindutva reduces social developments to questions of individual choice. Thus the Parivar aims to solve Hindu society's problems by inculcating 'correct

---

8. More detailed arguments on these points, and textual evidence from Hindutva texts to support them, can be found in Gopalakrishnan (2006).

values' in upper caste men, as exemplified by M.S. Golwalkar's declaration that "there is a 'crisis of character' in our country"; social problems are due to individuals' "demoniac ways" (Golwalkar 1979). Other Sangh Parivar leaders have made countless similar statements. The remaking of society depends on whether every person can be made a "good Hindu." What is a good Hindu is, in turn, defined by the Sangh.

- *The state exists* ***only*** *as the expression and guarantor of a collectivity founded around a transcendent principle*: The ideal state is the guarantor of the Hindu rashtra, a "nation" that exists as an organic and harmonious unity between "Hindus." The concept of "Hindu" here is linked on the one hand to the normative notion of the "good Hindu" discussed above, and on the other to the Sangh itself (see below). The Hindu nation is defined by the principles that it claims to adhere to. As Deendayal Upadhyaya (1979) once put it, "the state is brought into existence to protect the nation, and to maintain conditions in which the ideals of the nation can be translated into reality." These ideals constitute the nation's "soul", and the "laws that help manifest [this soul] are termed *dharma*." "A state cannot be without *dharma* nor can it be indifferent to *dharma*, just as fire cannot be without heat" (Upadhyaya 1979).
- *Divisions within this collectivity are unnecessary and pathological; the only division that is of importance is the line between "society" and its Other, the foreigner.* All divisions "within" society are the work of malignant outsiders or foreigners, aimed at breaking up the unity and harmony of the Hindu nation. Thus D.B. Thengadi once claimed that "in our system... [social sectors] form an infinite spiral with no inner conflicts and no tensions" (Thengadi 1979). Sangh leaders frequently draw analogies between society and the 'harmony' of the human body (see e.g. Golwalkar 1979).

As for those outside this nation, some of them are inferiors in need of education. As Golwalkar (1979) said, the RSS must "discourage people pursuing demoniac ways...[and inspire them] to develop their divine nature." This includes those too "ignorant" to understand their role in Hindu society, a description that is applied particularly to adivasis. But in case education does not work, Golwalkar continues, "we may have to use sanctions of force also in our endeavour." 'Outsiders' thus have a clear choice: they can swear allegiance to Hindutva and join 'society', or they can retain their beliefs, thereby confirming their 'foreignness' and making them fit for destruction.

- *It is the Sangh that both constitutes and represents the Hindu nation*. The Sangh is not merely an organisation of Hindus - it is the Hindu nation itself. As a Marathi textbook for *ekal vidyalaya* teachers puts it:
  "The aim of the Sangh is to organise the entire Hindu society, and not just to have a Hindu organisation within the ambit of this society. Had it been the latter, then the Sangh too would have added one more number to the already existing thousands of creeds. Though started as an institution, the aim of the Sangh is to expand so extensively that each and every individual and traditional social institutions like family, caste, profession, educational and religious institutions etc., are all to be ultimately engulfed into its system. The goal before the Sangh is to have an organised Hindu society in which all its constituents and institutions function in harmony and co-ordination, just as in the body organs"[9].

I have gone into these principles in some detail for two reasons. Firstly, there are strong resonances between these principles and neoliberalism, which will be discussed later. Secondly, and more importantly, there is a striking similarity between these tenets and the individualisation process that Poulantzas

9. This quote is taken from a textbook distributed to adivasi "acharyas" (teachers) in ekal vidyalayas in Thane District, Maharashtra.

outlines as one of the functions of the capitalist state. Hindutva, like most authoritarian ideologies, is as much about the production of an *essentialised individuality* as it is about a totalising notion of the state/community. Hindutva projects a vision of individuals as a collection of monads - "good Hindus" - with nothing to distinguish the one from the other, or to connect the one to the other, except a single legitimate collectivity: the Sangh. This is explicitly a *normative* vision, not a descriptive one. Such a society is the ideal, and it will be the effort of the Sangh to achieve it.

In this sense, Hindutva's understanding of the ideal society is in fact precisely the capitalist state's vision - reified to a level that it becomes unrecognisable within the parameters of bourgeois democracy.[10] And it was precisely at this level that the Hindutva ideological project was fundamentally opposed to the ideological bases of the other movements of the 1980s. It is arguable that Indian capital endorsed Hindutva because, as a hegemonic project, it directly sought the breaking down of the collectivities that the 1980s' movements had made the central feature of Indian politics. Such collectivities had become an increasing obstacle to the upholding of commodity relations as the organising principle of capitalist society.

It was this that translated into the vocal elite endorsement of the Sangh Parivar as a "nationalist" organisation, one pitted against "sectional" and "vested" interests. Most striking of all

---

10. I am not attempting to argue here that all capitalism is essentially authoritarian, or that all bourgeois democracies will inevitably culminate in fascism. Rather, I am extending Poulantzas' argument that representative democracy and the concept of human rights - counterposed to fascism and authoritarianism as the quintessential achievements of liberal capitalism - are in fact the result and the manifestation of class struggle (Poulantzas 1978). He argues that the class struggle, when expressed on the terrain of the capitalist state, is *manifested* in the form of individual rights. Thus there is no inbuilt check against authoritarianism in the capitalist state, but the very ubiquity of the class struggle means that the *actually existing* authoritarian states are the result of exceptional social configurations.

was the description of the Ayodhya movement as the creator of a "modern India" (Rajagopal 2001, BJP 1991). Indeed, contrary to much of the analysis of Hindutva as a "reaction" against "modernity", the Sangh and its cohorts have always been very clear that - in their vision - it is Hindutva itself that promotes "modernity" in India. And from the viewpoint of capital, this was correct, for it would indeed help to create that truly "modern" vision: an ideologically individualist society.

The Ayodhya Movement and Hindutva's Mass Base

Yet, while this argument may help explain the dominant interests being expressed by the project of Hindutva, we are still left with the question of how this project became *hegemonic* - or, more crudely, how it succeeded in building a mass base. For that, a closer examination of the Ayodhya movement is necessary.

There is no precise data on the nature of mass participation in the Ayodhya movement, but from available information it appears that its strongest bases were in urban areas, among the urban poor, and in small towns. Urban peripheries also saw strong participation, as well as some rural areas in Uttar Pradesh and Madhya Pradesh. However, it does not seem to have enjoyed a strong base in most rural areas. The organised working class in many urban areas supported the movement but were not active participants or leaders. Geographically the movement was most active in Maharashtra, Gujarat and the Hindi-speaking States, though it had support elsewhere as well.

Even this vague mapping throws up an interesting hypothesis: it appears that the Ayodhya movement mobilised precisely the social sectors that did not fully participate in the other 1980s' movements. But these sectors also included large numbers of petty commodity producers, particularly in the case of the urban poor. At this time of an increasing shift in favour of large capital, such persons were subject to the same intensifying reproduction squeeze as all other petty commodity producers. Further, they now included in their ranks the increasing numbers of those who lost formal employment as part of the first waves of liberalisation-induced deindustrialisation. At the time this was a geographically specific phenomenon, but one particularly striking example is the textile mills of Bombay and Ahmedabad - many of whose workers, at least in the case of Ahmedabad, subsequently became rabid supporters of the Sangh.

Yet, despite the fact that their circumstances were similar to those of the mass base of most of the 1980s' movements, these social sectors lacked political formations that could represent their demands in a time of increasing insecurity. One can hypothesise that two reasons fed into this vacuum. First, no corresponding social element to the "rich farmer" groups, which played the leading role elsewhere, existed in many of these contexts. Second, the state's role was also far more complex and indirect, particularly in urban areas. The populist articulation of a shared "community", led by large producers but with shared demands on the state, could hence not be formed. Producers were instead fragmented, directly facing the pressures of class differentiation and proletarianisation. Moreover, as the 1980s wore on, the inability of the other 1980s' movements to produce results for most of their members led increasingly to disillusionment even in areas where such movements were strong. It is indeed true that these social sectors faced a crisis; but it was a *political* crisis, not an *economic* one.

Building Mass Support

It is in this context that the Hindutva organisations undertook their mass expansion drive. Until this period, the Sangh had focused largely on cadre building and indoctrination as its main method of organisation. Such organising built a core of dedicated cadres with a large geographical reach, but could not undertake mass expansion, especially outside the caste and class lines that defined the traditional strongholds of the Parivar's organisations.

In the early part of the decade, the organisation undertook a series of changes. In particular, the RSS chose to foreground the VHP - and, later in the decade, the BJP - as the frontline Sangh Parivar organisations. Having been "relaunched" between 1979 and 1981, the VHP began a rapid expansion around 1984 (Jaffrelot 1999). The organisation led a series of mobilisations around the conversion of Dalits to Islam in Meenakshipuram (Tamil Nadu), the Shah Bano case, and the "Ekatmata Yatras." Mobilisation now began to revolve around temple-building, social service and the yatras, with the last becoming the primary mode of mass action. As Rajagopal (2001) puts it, "there was a shift away from sectarian view of organising, with indoctrination as its aim and daily drill as its chief method, to a far more pragmatic approach that emphasised mobilisation over indoctrination, and political effect over organisational discipline."

These new modes of organising had a very different impact from the old. They rested on offering various "gains" that corresponded to different contradictions facing different sectors. Unlike the other 1980s' movements, however, these "gains" were not about state support or political patronage. Instead, they were specifically geared towards concrete, immediate benefits and responses to the contradictions faced by these social sectors at the time.

Some examples are as follows. For adivasis in Madhya Pradesh - a community largely lacking in political organisation but nonetheless increasingly commoditised - the Vanvasi Kalyan Ashram offered direct access to hostels, schools, medical centres, etc. (and later became the nucleus of a more formal system of recruitment described in the last section). More than eight hundred schools were opened by the VHP in 1983 alone, mostly in tribal areas. Between 1978 to 1983, the number of full time activists in the VKA increased by six times, with most of their activities concerned with "service" (Jaffrelot 1999). Similar tactics were used with Dalits. Thus in the early 1980s, the VHP came out with a plan to build 100 temples in SC areas of Tamil Nadu (ibid.). Such temple building was to be a standard tactic throughout the decade, providing a way to channel funds into target areas and offering both employment and charity. In addition, for adivasis and Dalits specific economic contradictions with minorities were frequently exploited. One Ghaziabad riot in 1990, for instance, was triggered by the VHP essentially utilising a balmiki leader's tensions with Muslims over land in the outskirts of the town, the area to which both had been banished by caste Hindu pressures (Basu 1996). Meanwhile, on the other side of the caste spectrum, the urban upper caste youth who formed a significant proportion of the "shock troops" of the Parivar gained both employment/financial support and the ability to implicitly target the OBC mobilisation that threatened their access to state employment (Jaffrelot 1999, Basu 1996).

In addition to these direct material gains, the Sangh movement also offered a more intangible - but arguably still material - gain by creating new public spaces that were accessible to traditionally marginalised sectors. The movement offered access to higher steps on the social hierarchy by simultaneously aiming to retain its high caste character and "respectability" while allowing entry to those earlier excluded. This strategy was applied to various social sectors. Thus Dalits were specifically wooed by the VHP in the early 1980s; many of the new temples were specifically designed as public eating spaces for cross-caste meals. Dalits were also made carriers of the "holy water" in the Ekatmata Yatras (Jaffrelot 1999), and more generally both Dalits and lower castes were allowed access to ritual spaces traditionally denied to them (Rajagopal 2001).

For women, as is attested by a large body of literature on the gender aspects of Hindutva[11], such access to new spaces and possibilities of political action was perhaps the biggest attraction of the movement. The Sangh offered a "safe" avenue of political action that permitted women, particularly women of lower middle class households, to participate in politics without facing family opposition. Moreover it sometimes even raised, in a conservative and reactionary manner, issues such as sexual harassment and pornography (Basu 2001).

Such access to space leads both to a sense of *psychological* empowerment and also to more immediate gains, through membership in a privileged group including economically wealthy and powerful individuals. The VHP and VKA's networks in Madhya Pradesh, for instance, were largely funded

11. See for instance Jeffery and Basu (2001).

by local wealthy traders and former royal families. This was later added to by increasing donations from urban elites and from NRI's, who soon became a key funding source for the movement. The enormous amount of money that poured into the movement from such sources allowed them to offer both direct and indirect benefits to those who participated. Soon the VHP came to be known, in the RSS hierarchy, as the organisation aimed at the middle castes, the urban lower middle class, and similar social sectors of the kind described above.

Finally, during the latter half of this phase, access to these political spaces also meant participation in violence - and the financial, personal and psychological gains that follow on the use of violence against minority communities has been amply documented. Given the tilt of the state machinery towards the Hindutva organisations, such violence also often could be engaged in with impunity.

The Material-Ideological "Bargain"

In this sense, the movement offered both enhanced security and the prospect of social mobility. The ability to make these offers was crucially linked to the support given to the movement by capital, the state and the upper castes. None of these advantages could be offered by the other 1980s' movements, who did not enjoy such support.

But this was an offer that came with a bargain. The gains on offer accrued not to the class or the community, but to the *individual,* and the person had to self-constitute themselves as an *individual* by abandoning all other markers of identity. As seen above, acceptance of Hindutva ideology and organisational methods brought this as its strongest implication. Thus Dalits and adivasis were explicitly or implicitly forbidden to raise issues of discrimination against their communities. The Sangh women's organisations neither permitted nor encouraged raising of issues of women's rights (Sarkar 2001). In the present day, teachers in the Vanvasi Kalyan Ashram's ekal vidyalaya schools are asked to renounce any party affiliation, any caste identity and any commitment to any "sectional interest" other than that of "Bharat" (see below and

Gopalakrishnan and Sreenivasa 2007 for more details). In short, supporters and - at a much more intense level - cadres of the movement were required to discard all identities except their standing as an individual, "good Hindu."

The Commodification of Politics

Such methods of individualisation were then reinforced by wider discursive tactics of the movement itself. Rajagopal (1999) has argued that one of the key innovations of the Sangh Parivar in the 1980s was the conscious use of political *marketing*, the reconstitution of political action as *consumption*. The decision to utilise yatras as the most visible mobilisation vehicle was central to this strategy, and this was combined with the mass marketing of items like stickers, tridents, clothes and pictures. Available statistics show striking evidence of this. Jaffrelot (1999) notes how, in three days of the Ekatmata Yatra in 1983, 6,000 images of Bharat Mata and more than 70,000 bottles of "holy water" were sold. The Ram Shilanyas in 1989 was performed with the use of bricks sent by villages across the country, and involved a cash contribution of Rs. 1.25 by every individual who joined the ceremonies around the bricks. According to the VHP's statistics, more than 83 million rupees were collected. The yatras themselves became giant symbolic exercises, advertising the chosen few symbols of the movement (Ram; the trident; the colour saffron; the bricks) in a kind of mass cultural outpouring.

Political action in India has been historically associated with charismatic leadership, or at most with traditional party membership (as in the Communist organisations). The Ayodhya movement instead promoted a kind of *fetishisation* of such political relationships and of political action itself, converting one's relationship with a physical object or a symbol into the essence of one's relationship with the movement. Purchasing a sticker or a flag became a method of participating; participating in pujas for bricks and images was a mode of political mobilisation.

The use of symbols in this manner functioned synergistically with the expansion of corporate advertising and marketing into rural India, as both converged on the importance of the "brand" as a basis of action (Rajagopal 1999). The Hindutva movement explicitly tried to convert their politics into a "brand" - and endorsement of that brand through purchase, exhibition or worship constituted the act of political support for the movement. But what is a brand other than a reification of the commodity concept itself? In this way, the Ayodhya movement operated through a discourse of *commoditisation* of politics. Political action was integrated with *consumption.*

This analysis is not meant to claim that hate politics and Hindu chauvinism were irrelevant to the Hindutva mobilisation. They were no doubt the cultural categories and political tropes that formed the substance of the ideology. But the importance of the "Hindu community" was not a result of invocation of religious identity alone. Rather, this exploration postulates that it built on a partial satisfaction of the material-ideological needs of its cadre and its base - while simultaneously converting those needs into a driving force for individualisation and the restructuring of social relations in favour of capital. This partial coordination of interests between capital and large sections of petty commodity producers then becomes a dialectical part of the sense of "identity" of those involved. Hindu "identity" was thus politically *reconstructed* to mean individualised support for the movement, membership in its organisations and participation in its violence. In this sense, the movement was as much about rebuilding "Hindu" society as it was about targeting minorities.

6

THE ENTRY OF NEOLIBERALISM

The remainder of this paper concerns the Indian polity after the start of reforms in 1991, with the rise to total dominance of the neoliberal project in India. To evaluate the relationship between neoliberalism and Hindutva in this context, we have first to evaluate Indian neoliberalism itself, both as an economic phenomenon and as a political project.

There are in a sense two sides to Indian neoliberalism. On the one hand, the glaring triumph of neoliberal policies and their endorsement by practically all major political parties across the political spectrum indicates the strength of neoliberal ideology as a shaping force of state action in the country. This is the analysis that most of us on the left share, and it reflects the massive defeats inflicted on the left in the last two decades.

But at the same time, Indian neoliberalism has some peculiar weaknesses. One such weakness is reflected in the policy trajectory that neoliberalism has taken in India. In the first decade, the primary focus was on regulatory liberalisation, trade liberalisation, capital account liberalisation and state rollback - namely the "classical" neoliberal model followed in most nations. But such reforms, essentially aimed at strengthening the power of finance capital, ran into growing obstacles. Those that remained confined to finance and industrial spheres, such as capital account liberalisation, went ahead with relatively fewer hitches. Others that were essentially reallocation of resources within the state, such as budget cuts, also have proceeded rapidly. But those that directly affected petty commodity producers, or the small number of capitalist producers in the agricultural sector - such as food subsidies, the public procurement and distribution system, or complete import liberalisation - have been partly or completely blocked. The PDS has been converted into the "targeted PDS" and thus severely maimed, but it has not been dismantled. Similarly tariff cuts have greatly harmed agricultural producers, but they have not been as total as they were in many other parts of the world.

It is arguable that this weakness reflects the nature of Indian capitalism and the continuing relationship between Indian capital and petty commodity producers. The existence of petty commodity producers is simultaneously a requirement for and a fetter on Indian capitalism, both as a result of democratic politics and through its material relationship with capital. Indeed, the vast majority of production in India, even that in the so-called organised sector, involves some degree of involvement of petty commodity producers. In this sense, incidentally, the neoliberal emphasis on informalisation and "outsourcing" is hardly new to Indian capitalism.

Hence, neoliberalism has required a recalibration in India. This recalibration has become increasingly apparent in the last seven or eight years. In this period, the major new initiatives in Indian neoliberalism have been in the area of what David Harvey (2003) described as "accumulation by dispossession" (or "accumulation by encroachment", to refer to Prabhat Patnaik's (2005) slightly more accurate description of events in India). These include liberalisation of mining, the accelerated growth in infrastructure sectors, privatisation of natural resources, and the creation of Special Economic Zones. Also in this category are the brutal judiciary-driven assaults on forest dwellers, urban workers and urban petty traders/producers. As is argued by the theory of accumulation by dispossession, these initiatives are aimed at directly expropriating petty commodity producers (as well as subsistence producers, in a few contexts) rather than eliminating them through market forces. By forcibly stripping these producers of their means of production, they result in mass proletarianisation and super-accumulation for the beneficiary capitals.

Unlike the blocked "reforms", however, such moves towards accumulation by dispossession are unlikely to lead to the elimination of most, or even a significant portion, of petty commodity producers. They still only affect a relatively small number of producers as compared to the Indian economy as a whole. Rather than an effort at destroying petty commodity production, they can more accurately be seen as the most visible vanguard of a drive for intensified extraction of surplus from the latter - a drive whose most widespread manifestation is the crisis of reproduction in agriculture. This crisis, while also accelerating proletarianisation among the poor peasantry, is impacting producers in direct proportion to the degree of their commoditisation - meaning that the so-called "middle peasantry", who were simultaneously the most vulnerable and the most commoditised, are being hit the hardest.

Thus, whereas petty commodity production cannot be totally eliminated, it can be more intensely subjugated and made more vulnerable to intensified extraction. Under neoliberalism, Indian capitalism has proven to prefer a more shrunken, dominated space for petty commodity production than in the earlier model. This intensified extraction is in turn made possible by the shift in capital accumulation towards larger producers and the organised sector. It is in this context that the political project of neoliberalism has developed.

Indian Neoliberalism as a Political Project

The failure to implement the "typical" package of neoliberal reforms in India is only one facet of Indian neoliberalism's weakness. The other becomes immediately apparent if we compare India to Thatcherite Britain, Reagan's America, or the Latin American dictatorships. In India, neoliberalism is not a mass political project. No political party or organised political force (such as the army in Latin America) has adopted neoliberalism *as such* as a part of its ideology. To this day, with the very significant exception of Gujarat (to which we will return), no political party has won elections with anything resembling an open endorsement of neoliberal policies. Moreover, other than a generic celebration of consumption and consumption-fuelled aspirations, even popular vernacular media rarely articulates the ideological principles of neoliberalism.[12]

Indian neoliberalism has thus largely failed to build itself into a truly hegemonic project. This is in sharp contrast to Thatcherism, for instance, which built a popular base by using neoliberal ideology to refract genuine contradictions of social democracy (Hall 1979).

In Gramsci's terms, Indian neoliberalism lacks a "totalitarian party"; it is an ideology without an organisation, except parts of the state machinery itself.

Why this is the case is a far larger question. At an ideological level, by comparison with Thatcherism, it can be seen that the contradictions experienced by most Indians cannot be easily reduced to the formulae of state over-regulation. The continued presence of the state as both supporter and opponent of petty production prevents an easy attack on it as an external imposition. The discourses of the 1980s remain far too powerful to be swept aside, giving rise to endless laments from neoliberal ideologues about "vote bank" politics and the inability of the Indian masses to understand the wisdom of the "market."

This political failure in turn becomes an obstacle to the subjugation of petty producers. It is clear that if Indian capital found the discourses of the 1980s' movements a fetter on their expansion, neoliberalism does so at a far more intense level. Such politics directly opposes the blanket liberalisation, regulatory withdrawal and speculative freedom that are so central to the neoliberal project. Moreover, in the Indian context, the persistence of such politics blocks the wholesale subjugation of petty commodity producers and hinders the ability of capital to impose its will on the Indian polity. As such, if neoliberalism is to politically succeed in reshaping India's society and polity as it wishes, it requires a stronger foundation on which to attack such politics.

12. With the exception of some films such as *Guru* or the Tamil blockbuster *Sivaji*.

7

RELATIONS BETWEEN NEOLIBERALISM AND HINDUTVA

It is at this point that it becomes apparent that neoliberalism has a strong common agenda with the other project discussed here - Hindutva. This is not in any sense to downplay the obvious differences and tensions between the two projects (most centrally around their conceptions of "freedom"). It also bears repeating that this does not imply that an alliance between the two was or is "inevitable." Yet, as living political projects, shaped in a dialectical relationship with their social foundations, their common goals offer a space that can be exploited. It is from this perspective that we can understand the gradual growth of the alliance between Hindutva and neoliberalism that developed over the 1990s.

How does such an alliance operate? A good starting point is to note discursive dynamics in the English media. As an ideological site largely internal to the ruling class, the English media is an ideal location for ruling class organic intellectuals to play out negotiations between ideological projects. By observing media discourse, we can then identify the degree to which political projects are finding shared ground.

It is hence striking to note that over the last fifteen years, the English media has shifted to strongly emphasise the ideological resonances between neoliberalism, Hindutva and individualisation. This can be seen if, in a similar manner to the outline of Hindutva conceptions made above, we also outline the conceptions of neoliberalism on these issues:

- *Reduction of social processes to individual choice*: In neoliberal ideology, all action in all social spheres is built around "utility-maximising" individuals. Despite being portrayed as a descriptive concept, this is in fact a normative one. The 'failure' of individuals to behave as "rational" utility maximisers is attributed to "perverse incentives" from either state or society, which is condemned as both immoral and irrational. In this sense, the utility maximising individual is the equivalent of the "good Hindu" in Hindutva - both the centre of the social order and the ideal that that order aspires to produce.
- *The state exists as the expression and guarantor, not of individual or collective rights, but of a supreme principle*: The place of Hindu rashtra is in this case taken by "the market". The ideal state is the night watchman, the guarantor of the "market" - the only legitimate collective social activity. The state should ideally be the market's guarantor against interference, nothing less and nothing more. In fact, it is particularly striking that one finds precisely the same phrase - "night watchman" - being used by the Sangh intellectual Dattopant Thengadi (1979) to describe the state.
- *Divisions within society are unnecessary and pathological; the only division that is of importance is the line between "society" and its Other.* In neoliberalism, "civil society" - the social counterpart of the economic concept of the "market" - is the only legitimate social institution (a concept taken even further with the notion of "social capital"). As in Hindutva, classes, castes and other identities are fictions, with their roots in malign state interference and "political meddling." In neoliberalism, the state itself takes the place of the "foreigner." Welfare agencies, the bureaucracy, the legislature, political parties - all are 'outside' society and responsible for its "pathological" divisions. Political actors are socially illegitimate, and for both Hindutva and the neoliberals there is no worse crime than to "politicise" social issues.

Simply listing these principles already makes it apparent that they have become shrill themes in much English media coverage. Perhaps the best example is the reservations "debate." Caste-based reservations are attacked on the ground that they violate the principles of individual "merit", as per the first principle. Since the state's role is to guarantee these principles and not interfere with them, the state is attacked for "meddling" with "meritocracy" rather than doing its job and providing infrastructure, education, etc. Finally, the reservations policy is attacked for "dividing" society along "caste lines" and its roots are seen as being "vote bank" politics. Yet, even though it would be totally contrary to neoliberal principles, much of the English media is happy to advocate economic reservations - which have long formed part of the individualised "social uplift" agenda preached by the Sangh Parivar, projecting reservations as charity rather than social justice. This inconsistency is a hallmark of the effort at finding shared ground.

In an earlier paper[13], I have explored other examples of how these principles play out in operation. Moreover, the media is not only concerned with emphasising the common areas between the two agendas - it has also become a site for de-emphasising and reshaping those aspects that are not in harmony between the two projects. Thus, both in the view of the media and in reality, the Sangh Parivar has backpedaled on those of its issues that are not of interest to neoliberals: swadeshi, most of all, but also such issues as Akhand Bharat, Article 370, the universal civil code, etc. The Sangh's earlier emphasis on "austerity" has also been quietly forgotten. The media in turn projects this as the gradual "moderation" of the Hindutva forces as they join the "mainstream."

Similar policy accommodations on the part of neoliberal ideologues are also visible on a close reading. Some of them include:

- The continual and peculiar emphasis in Indian neoliberalism on "national self-confidence." This is foreign to neoliberal ideology as such. Rather, it is a

13. Gopalakrishnan (2006).

notion that clearly owes a great deal to Hindutva's promotion of the concept of a "national self" that is weakened and sapped by its internal divisions. It is not an accident that exactly the same terminology - "awakening", "newfound confidence", "assertiveness" - that was used by the Sangh Parivar to describe the Ayodhya movement is now used by neoliberals to describe India post 1991.

- The endorsement of economic reservations, as described above.
- The attitude towards NRI's, seen as a kind of "vanguard" of both projects. NRI's are projected as ideal Indians, representatives of what 'India' could achieve if Indians were 'good' individuals following correct social 'values'. There could hardly be any message that neoliberalism and Hindutva agree upon more.

An Institutional and Political Alliance

These discursive adjustments form the face of a much deeper and growing relationship.[14] Such collaboration reached its most visible form at the national level during the NDA regime, when the Sangh Parivar and neoliberal ideologues cooperatively attempted to develop political praxis, institutional structures and hegemonic ideologies that allowed them to reap the advantages of a mutual alliance.

Among these moves were the accelerated privatisation of education, intensified repression of social movements and the opening of the Indian economy to NRI-driven foreign investment. The two projects also promoted "anti-terrorism" as the single most important agenda of the Indian state, while attempting to dissolve its commitment to any forms of "social justice". The 2004 election campaign, with its celebration of "India Shining", was a particularly evocative reflection of this

14. I have made a more detailed exploration of some examples of these principles have playing out in the English media elsewhere (Gopalakrishnan 2006).

alliance - India was shining because it was "growing" both economically and in "self-confidence" as a Hindu nation.

Meanwhile the Sangh Parivar, utilising its access to even enormous amounts of funds (significant amounts of which were either state or foreign-generated), institutionalised and formalised the "bargain" described above. The new pattern of expansion relied on the Sangh's "seva" arms, which expanded enormously during the NDA regime. By the end of the NDA period, Vidya Bharati, the RSS educational organisation, was running - and still continues to run - the country's largest private school network. Sangh Parivar outfits emerged as the largest "NGO's" working in the tribal areas (Vanvasi Kalyan Ashram and its allies). In Orissa and in Gujarat, cadre recruitment grew on a massive scale through "relief" operations in the wake of the 1999 cyclone and the 2001 earthquake respectively.[15]

A key example of these new practices is the "ekal vidyalayas" in tribal areas, possibly the largest Sangh Parivar cadre recruitment activity today.[16] As per their website, there are 26,314 ekal vidyalayas in operation at the time of writing[17], but the actual number is likely to be far larger. In these schools, young tribal men and women are hired as acharyas (teachers), given brief 'training' and a curriculum, and asked to take regular classes for children out of school. In practice, neither the curriculum nor the training nor the student population is clear. There is no infrastructure other than irregular textbooks. Even where the acharya ceases to function, they at times carry on drawing their salary.

As such, the schoolchildren do not seem to be the target of the scheme. Rather, the acharyas themselves appear to be the main goal. One obvious attraction is the stable salary (between Rs. 300 and Rs. 500). Second, the appeals in the training are

---

15. For more details, see "In Bad Faith: British Charity and Hindu Extremism", by AWAAZ - South Asia Watch. Available online at http://www.awaazsaw.org/ibf/index.htm
16. More details on this can be found in Gopalakrishnan and Sreenivasa (2007).
17. http://ekalindia.org , last accessed on July 5th, 2008.

mostly not concerned with overt Hindutva or even Hindu appeals. Instead, the focus is on social service, the need for *gaon vikas,* and the problems of "division" introduced by 'politics'. The youth are forbidden to join any political party or any social movement of the area. The stress of the ekal vidyalaya progam is on apolitical social service - which in our society is a high status occupation. Thus the program offers a combination of *material security* through the salary, and of *social mobility* by earning respect of those with higher social stature while participating in a high status social occupation.

But, once again, the "bargain" requires the acharya to choose individualisation and depoliticisation, except through their commitment to the Sangh. Thus, ekal vidyalayas and other Sangh 'seva' activities build a committed grassroots cadre for whom the "bargain" mentioned earlier is now given a formal, very concrete form: benefits to *individuals* who perform, and the fear of the loss of all such benefits and a return to being a 'non-entity' if one fails.

Such a cadre in turn benefits Indian capital in general and neoliberalism in particular, in exchange for which funds are provided, media access guaranteed and state support (even under the UPA) more or less constant. The result is to make it easier to counter a 1980s' style of politics, greatly weakening the capacity of petty commodity producers to resist the attack on their livelihoods.

2004 and After

The experiment was partly cut short by the 2004 elections. However hegemonic the aspirations of the neoliberal-Hindutva alliance were, it had failed to achieve real hegemony in the electoral realm. But its successor, the UPA, has become a classic instance of a neoliberal regime that is not backed by an organised political force. It has pursued a schizophrenic political program, whose contradictions have offered space for some small popular gains along with an avalanche of neoliberal policies. It will also almost certainly become an example of how Indian neoliberalism, in the absence of a "totalitarian" party as its ally, devours the support base of its own regime.

A sharp contrast to this situation is the 2007 Gujarat elections, where arguably the Sangh-neoliberal alliance has had its first major and resounding victory. Bankrolled by big capital, publicly proclaimed to be the saviour of both business and nation, the Sangh rode to power against a fragmented opposition speaking the language and raising the issues of the 1980s - caste divides, farmers' suicides and tribal distress, in addition to tokenistic 'secularism.' The Gujarat verdict was built around two simultaneous phenomena. The first was the total dominance of capital, with state support, over both the working class and petty commodity producers, who are at the mercy of big capital in the State. The resulting insecurity and constant sense of threat was fed off of by the Sangh, whose "bargain" became evermore attractive in this context. The result was the Sangh-driven organisational destruction of all other political formations, whose cadres were poached or coopted into Sangh formations (those who would not, or could not, were repressed or killed). In this context, there was no serious opposition; the Sangh has indeed effectively achieved hegemony, and the totalitarian party has reached fruition.

This is not the only form these collaborations have taken. In Chhattisgarh, a different kind of collaboration has created Salwa Judum, a state supported militia formed by an unholy alliance between the security forces, the Vanvasi Kalyan Ashram (whose cadres are known to be closely involved) and corporate pressure for mineral extraction. Operating in the southern districts of Dantewada and Bijapur, the Salwa Judum has killed hundreds of adivasis and driven lakhs of people from their homes in the name of fighting the Maoists. The militia is mostly led by the elite among the adivasi communities of the area, those who are, in that sense, most commoditised and most accessible to the offers made by the state/Sangh/capital combine. Even as per official figures, more than 600 villages have been emptied of their population; their residents have either fled into the jungles or are trapped in horrific "relief camps" being run by the State government. There are credible allegations that at least part of the motivation for doing this is to ease the handing over of the land to mining corporations.

Wiping out the Maoists, among the most dangerous defenders of petty commodity and subsistence production, is no doubt also a goal for Indian capital - and of course for the Sangh.

Whereas Gujarat is India's most capitalist state, Chhattisgarh is probably among the least. A truly hegemonic form of this alliance cannot take place here, for the degree of commoditisation is insufficient. Hence the balance within hegemony shifts towards force and away from consent, and the form it takes is that of direct, brutal violence - accumulation by dispossession in the most inhuman manner.

8

CONCLUSION AND IMPLICATIONS FOR LEFT PRAXIS

Neither of these experiments is immediately replicable at the national level, but we do left politics a serious disservice if we therefore dismiss the danger. We have long allowed ourselves to be comforted with descriptions of the Indian right as peddlers of false notions, fraudulent demagogues building castles in the air around "Hindu rashtra" and "India Shining." In particular, we have believed that Hindutva is primarily an exercise in identity-based chauvinism, a hate politics targeting minorities through propaganda and disinformation. We have seen our role in tackling this threat as primarily being one of awareness raising, enlightenment and education.

The argument here has been that this interpretation of historical processes is incorrect. The Sangh in particular has achieved its incredible growth because it is a truly totalitarian party of the ruling class: responding to the needs of multiple social sectors, while presenting solutions to those needs in forms that correspond to the interests of the ruling classes. Fighting such projects cannot be limited to awareness raising alone. They must be confronted as *organisations*, to hinder and undermine their ability to offer the material-ideological 'bargain' that operates at their very foundation.

When the UPA government falls in 2009, as it is almost certain to do, there will be another chance for neoliberal-Hindutva alliances to explore their full possibilities at the national level. The situation is ripe for such politics to blossom again. At this time, if we do not fight the Sangh on the political level, we not only hinder the battle for 'secularism', we provide Indian neoliberalism with an extremely powerful ally. One can even speculate that the one cannot be defeated without at least weakening the other.

9

BIBLIOGRAPHY

Basu, Amrita (1996). "Mass Movement or Elite Conspiracy? The Puzzle of Hindu Nationalism", in David Ludden (ed.) *Making India Hindu*. New Delhi: Oxford University Press.

Bernstein, Henry (2001). "'The Peasantry' in Global Capitalism: Who, Where and Why?", *Socialist Register 2001*.

Bernstein, Henry (2003). "Farewell to the Peasantry", *Transformation* 52. Durban: University of Kwa-Zulu Natal.

Bharatiya Janata Party (BJP) (1991). Election Manifesto 1991. New Delhi: Bharatiya Janata Party.

Chatterjee, Partha (1998). "Development Planning and the Indian State", in T.J. Byres (ed.) *The State, Development Planning and Liberalisation in India*. New Delhi: Oxford University Press.

Corbridge, Stuart and John Harriss (2000). *Reinventing India: Liberalisation, Hindu Nationalism and Popular Democracy*. Cambridge: Polity Press.

Dhanagare, D.N. (1995). "The Class Character and Politics of Farmers' Movement in Maharashtra during the 1980s", in Tom Brass (ed.) *New Farmers' Movements in India*. Essex: Frank Cass.

Ghosh, Jayati and C.P. Chandrasekhar (2000). *The Market That Failed*. New Delhi: Leftword.

Golwalkar, M.S. ('Guruji') (1979). "Integral Man", in D. Upadhyaya, M.S. Golwalkar and D.B. Thengadi. *The Integral Approach*. New Delhi: Deendayal Research Institute.

Gopalakrishnan, Shankar (2006). "Defining, Constructing and Policing a 'New India': Exploring the Relationship Between Neoliberalism and Hindutva", *Economic and Political Weekly*, June 30.

Gopalakrishnan, Shankar and Priya Sreenivasa (2007). "Carnivorous

Flower: Bringing Adivasis Within the 'Communal' Fold", *Combat Law,* May - June. New Delhi: Human Rights Law Network.

Gramsci, Antonio (1971). *Selections from the Prison Notebooks.* London: Lawrence and Wishart.

Hall, Stuart (1979). "The Great Moving Right Show", *Marxism Today,* January.

Harriss-White, Barbara (2003). *India Working: Essays on Society and Economy.* Cambridge: Cambridge University Press.

Harriss-White, Barbara and Nandini Gooptu (2001). "Mapping India's World of Unorganized Labour", *Socialist Register 2001.*

Harvey, David (2003). "New Imperialism: Accumulation By Dispossession", *Socialist Register 2004,* pp. 63-87.

Jaffrelot, Christopher (1999). *The Hindu Nationalist Movement and Indian Politics.* New Delhi: Penguin India.

Jeffery, Patricia and Amrita Basu (eds.) (2001). *Resisting the Sacred and the Secular: Women's Activism and Politicised Religion in South Asia.* New Delhi: Kali for Women.

Patnaik, Prabhat (2005). "The Economics of the New Phase of Imperialism", August 26. Available online at http://www.macroscan.com/anl/aug05/pdf/Economics_New_Phase.pdf.

Poulantzas, Nicos (1978). *State, Power, Socialism.* Paris: Presses Universitaires de France. (Tr. Patrick Camiller, reprinted by Verso in 2000).

Rajagopal, Arvind (1999). "Brand Logics and the Cultural Forms of Political Society in India", *Social Text,* 17:3.

Rajagopal, Arvind (2001). *Politics After Television: Religious Nationalism and the Reshaping of the Indian Public.* Cambridge: Cambridge University Press.

Rodrik, Dani and Subramaniam, Arvind (2004). "From 'Hindu Growth' to Productivity Surge: The Mystery of the Indian Growth Transition", NBER Working Paper 10376, March.

Sarkar, Tanika (2001). "Women, Community and Nation", in Patricia Jeffery and Amrita Basu (eds.) *Resisting the Sacred and the Secular: Women's Activism and Politicised Religion in South Asia.* New Delhi: Kali for Women.

Thengadi, D.B. (1979). "Integral Humanism - A Study", in D. Upadhyaya, M.S. Golwalkar and D.B. Thengadi. *The Integral Approach.* New Delhi: Deendayal Research Institute.

Upadhyaya, Deenadayal (1979). "Integral Humanism", in D. Upadhyaya, M.S. Golwalkar and D.B. Thengadi. *The Integral Approach*. New Delhi: Deendayal Research Institute.

Upadhyaya, Deenadayal (1979b). "Harmony Between the Individual and the Collectivity", in D. Upadhyaya, M.S. Golwalkar and D.B. Thengadi. *The Integral Approach*. New Delhi: Deendayal Research Institute.

Vanaik, Achin (1990). *The Painful Transition: Bourgeois Democracy in India*. London: Verso.